WORLD RELIGIONS

DAVID SELF

A LION BOOK

Published by
Lion Publishing plc
Sandy Lane West, Oxford, England
ISBN 0 7459 3603 2
Albatross Books Pty Ltd
PO Box 320, Sutherland, NSW 2232, Australia
ISBN 0 7324 1454 7

First edition 1996
10 9 8 7 6 5 4 3 2 1 0

Acknowledgments

Photographs
Andes Press Agency: /Dave and Ceri Hill spreads 6 (above right), 7 (above
right); /Carlos Reyes Manzo spreads 2 (above right), 3 (below left, below right),
4 (below centre), 5 (above centre), 6 (centre left, below right), 7 (centre left), 9
(centre right, above centre), 10 (centre right, below right), 11 (below far right),
16 (above centre), 20 (centre left, centre far right); /Irit Sapir spread 12 (above
right corner)
Susanna Burton: spreads 4 (above left), 7 (below right), 8 (below centre), 10
(above centre), 14 (centre left, above centre), 16 (below right), 18 (centre left),
19 (below centre, centre right, centre left)
Sonia Halliday Photographs: spreads 2 (centre right), 13 (centre far left)
The Hutchison Library: spreads 5 (below right), 6 (above right), 11 (below
centre); /Nancy Durrell McKenna spread 8 (below right)
Images of India/Dinodia Picture Agency: spreads 5 (centre far left), 12 (above
right), 17 (above centre); /Roderick Johnson spread 17 (above right);
/C. Milind, A. Ketkar spread 20 (centre right)
The John Robert Young Collection: spreads 15 (below left), 16 (centre right)
Link Picture Library/Orde Eliason: spread 19
Lion Publishing: spreads 2 (centre left), 11 (below left), 14 (above centre), 15
(centre right), 19 (above right); /David Alexander spreads 3 (far left), 4 (above
centre), 13 (below right), 14 (below left), 17 (below centre left), 18 (above
right), 20 (below centre right); /David Townsend spreads 2 (below left), 5
(below centre), 15 (above left), 17 (below left, below centre right), 19 (above
centre)
The MacQuitty International Photographic Collection: spread 2 (above left)
© Ann & Bury Peerless – Slide Resources & Picture Library: spreads 3 (centre
right), 17 (centre left)
Nigel Poulton: spread 14 (above centre)
Z. Radovan, Jerusalem: spreads 8 (centre far left), 9 (centre left)
Lois Rock: spread 10 (below left, inset below left)
Nicholas Rous: spread 1 (above left)
Peter Sanders Photography: spreads 2 (below right), 3 (above right), 4 (above
right), 6 (centre right), 8 (centre left), 9 (below right), 13 (centre far right), 14
(above right), 17 (below right corner), 20 (above centre)
Setu Graphics/K. Ahmad: spreads 11 (above right), 16 (centre left, below left),
17 (centre right)
Doug Sewell: spread 10 (centre left)
Clifford Shirley (Fotomedia): spread 4 (centre left)
Skjold Photographs: spreads 5 (above right), 8 (above right), 18 (below centre),
20 (centre right)
Mr & Mrs John Wheeler: spread 13 (centre left)
John Williams Studios: spreads 1 (below left, above right), 2 (above left, far
right), 3 (above centre), 4 (below left [angels © Jan Barger], below right), 5
(centre right), 6 (below left), 8 (below left, centre right), 9 (below left, below
centre, above right corner), 10 (below left corner, above left/centre, above right
corner), 11 (above centre, centre right), 12 (above left, centre left, below right,
below left), 15 (below right), 16 (above right), 18 (above left, far right)
Estate of Yigael Yadin: spread 13 (below right corner)
Zefa Pictures: spreads 12 (below right corner), 15 (above centre), 16 (above
left corner), 17 (above left corner)

Illustrations
Illustration on cover (and elsewhere) by Simon Bull
Maps and diagrams by Oxford Illustrators (except for the symbols on spread 1
and elsewhere)

Contents

1 How amazing!

Since time began, people have looked at the world around them and *wondered*. How does it all happen? How did it all begin?

Have you ever seen a sunrise... with the golden sunlight scattering the dull grey night?

Questions, questions

Who made the sky, the sun and all the other stars... who makes spring happen each year, bringing new life to a world that seems dead and cold? Is it part of a *plan* that a tiny seed grows into a beautiful plant, providing food for animals and people?

Many people believe that it must all have been made by a special being—a being they call 'God'. They say that God existed before the world and all the universe. They say that God knows about everything that happens in the world and in space. God is invisible, they say, but people can see God's work in the beauty of the sunrise, in the beauty of a tiny flower—and in many other things.

Who believes?

People have believed in a great being for thousands of years. Today, believers can be found all over the world. They include people of all kinds—children, grown-ups, men, women, people with little or no schooling and university professors...

Professor Sir Bernard Lovell is a scientist who has spent his working life studying the stars. Much of the time, he used a radio telescope which let him see very distant and very faint stars. He became certain that the universe (including our own world) did not happen by accident.

'Discoveries have shown that even if conditions near the very beginning of the universe were only very slightly different from what they were, then we could not exist.'

This has led him to believe that there must be a God who made it all happen.

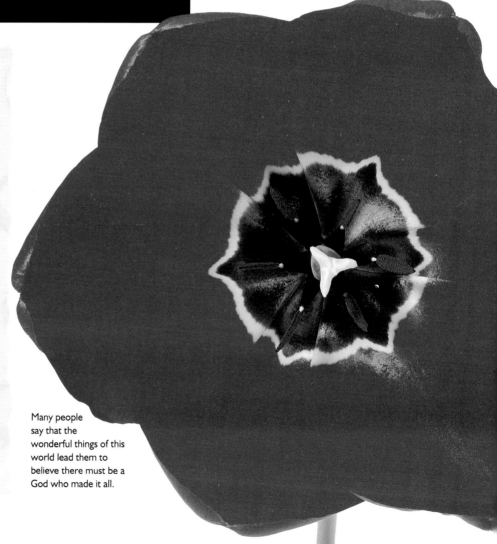

Many people say that the wonderful things of this world lead them to believe there must be a God who made it all.

Many faiths

People who believe in God are called 'religious'. What they believe about God is their 'religion' or 'faith'.

There are many religions in the world. They all started in different ways, at different times and in different places. Here are six that have a lot of influence in today's world.

Faiths around the world

Once upon a time, people who followed each religion stayed in their own part of the world. But as people began to travel more, each religion spread to other countries. Now there are followers of several religions in nearly every country of the world.

Have you ever held a flower in your hand and marvelled at the beauty that unfolds from a tiny brown seed?

The symbols of the great faiths

Hinduism

Some of the oldest religions began in India. One is called Hinduism.

The symbol of Hinduism is the OM or AUM. It symbolises what people cannot imagine, Brahman.

Buddhism

Buddhism is a very ancient philosophy from India. A philosophy is a way of understanding the world—making sense of it (◊10).

The eight-spoked wheel is the symbol of Buddhist teaching.

Judaism

Another very old religion is the one followed by Jewish people. It began in what people now call the Middle East and is called Judaism. Jewish people believe that long ago God gave them their own special country. It is now called Israel, and its most important city is Jerusalem (◊17).

The Star of King David—the greatest king in the history of the Jewish people—is the most widely used symbol; but the seven-branched candlestick, the menorah, is the official symbol of Israel.

Sikhism

Another religion called Sikhism began in India. It began much later than the other major world religions.

The Khanda is the name of the two-edged sword, symbolising God's concern for truth and justice.

Islam

Islam is another important religion that also started in the Middle East. It began six hundred years after the birth of Jesus.

For people of hot desert countries who often travel by night when it is cool, the stars are their guide while the moon lights their way. Islam guides and lights its followers on the journey of life.

Christianity

Two thousand years ago a Jewish man named Jesus was born. He did many wonderful things and attracted a number of followers. These followers believed he was sent by God, and called him 'the Chosen One' or 'the Anointed One'. The Greek word for this is 'Christ'. Followers of 'Jesus Christ' are called Christians.

The cross is a reminder that Jesus Christ was put to death on a cross—and of the belief that he suffered and died on behalf of all people, and rose to new life.

Follow the signs

In this book, each of the symbols of the six faiths has been linked to the colour shown here. To find out about one particular faith, look for headings which show its symbol and colour.

Do you know?

The arrow and page number signs (◊1) in this book tell you where to turn to find out more about a topic.

The beginnings of some religions are lost in the mists of time. In other cases, however, one person is highly regarded by followers of the religion as the one who shaped the way they understand the world.

Small beginnings

Five of the faiths on this page can be traced to small—and fragile—beginnings centred on one person and a tiny band of followers. Yet they have grown and grown, and provided wisdom and inspiration for many people over hundreds of years—like a tiny seedling growing to a mighty tree.

Hinduism

This religion is so ancient that no one knows when it began—much less if any one person began it. Hinduism is rooted firmly in the traditions of India.

Hindu god

A statue of one of the many gods of Hinduism

The Buddha

The founder of Buddhism was an Indian prince called Siddhartha Gautama (later known as the Buddha). He lived about five hundred years before Jesus. He grew up in a splendid palace but when he saw how many people suffered from old age and illnesses, he gave up all his wealth and wandered the countryside. At last, he sat down under a great tree, trying to decide what was *really* important, what was 'the truth'. He then taught what he had learned to others (↻12).

This statue of the Buddha shows him looking painfully thin—emaciated. Siddhartha Gautama gave up all bodily comforts in his quest for truth.

Jesus

Jesus was a Jew, born about two thousand years ago in Palestine—the region of present-day Israel. He grew up in a town called Nazareth where he worked as a carpenter. When he was thirty, he collected together a small group of followers—'disciples'. They went with him as he travelled round the country. He attracted crowds wherever he went because he was able to heal people with a touch and do other miraculous things. He also told people about God and about God's love for the world. To do so, he often used stories about everyday things. These stories are sometimes called parables.

For Christians, the most important event in the life of Jesus is what happened after his death in Jerusalem (↻18).

Abraham and Moses

Jewish people regard a man named Abraham as the 'grandfather' of their nation. Long ago—close on four thousand years ago—Abraham believed God promised to give him many descendants. They became the people of Israel, later known as the Jews. God would do good things for them and through them would do good things to all the world.

One other important person in the history of the Jewish people is Moses. He was a great leader who helped Abraham's descendants escape from slavery in Egypt and travel to a land where they could live in freedom, obeying God's laws.

Moses and the law

According to the Jewish scriptures, God gave the people of Israel laws to live by. They are said to have been given to Moses here at Mount Sinai.

The Ten Gurus

A man named Nanak was the first teacher of the religion now known as Sikhism. He was born on 15 April 1469 in a village called Talwandi in what is now Pakistan.

The people in that area were either Hindus or Muslims. Nanak saw good in both these religions and said all people were brothers in God's eyes. He spent his life travelling and teaching and he became known as Guru Nanak. ('Guru' means teacher.)

After Guru Nanak, there were nine more Sikh Gurus. The last of these, Guru Gobind Singh, founded the Brotherhood of all Sikhs which is known as the Khalsa.

Jesus' story of the Lost Coin

There was a woman who had ten very valuable silver coins. One day, she lost one of them. Because she lived in a house which had few windows, she lit a lamp so she could see properly and swept the floor of her house carefully. When she found the coin, she was so excited she told all her friends and neighbours: 'It's good news! I've found the coin I lost!'

Jesus told the people who were listening that God is just as pleased when a person who has been doing wrong things and living apart from God turns to live in the way God wants.

Jesus

No one really knows what Jesus looked like. However, many different pictures have been made of him in the two thousand years since he lived. This one dates from about eight hundred years ago.

A cave on Mount Hira

A cave on Mount Hira where Muhammad is said to have received messages from an angel. It overlooks the city of Mecca.

The Prophet Muhammad

For Muslims, the followers of the religion Islam, the most important teacher is the Prophet Muhammad. He worked as a trader in the city of Mecca. When he wanted to feel close to God, he would go north to a hill called Mount Hira and especially to a cave, high up in the mountain. There he could be alone and there he could think.

One night, when he was in the cave, he heard a voice. In front of him stood an angel who gave him a message. After this, the angel appeared often to Muhammad, giving him messages which he was to repeat to those people of Mecca who would listen to what he had to tell them. And Muhammad taught them the message of the angel— that there is only one God, whose name is God (or, in Arabic, 'Allah').

When Muslims use the name of their Prophet, they usually follow it with the blessing 'Peace be upon him'—sometimes shown in print as 'the Prophet Muhammad 鑅'.

Holy books

Almost every religion has at least one holy book in which arc written down the things that are important about that religion.

✡ The Jewish Bible

Among the Jewish holy books is a collection of 39 books which are called the Tenakh or Jewish 'Bible'. They are divided into three groups:

● **The Torah** (sometimes called the Five Books of Moses). These books describe the early history of the Jewish people (or Israelites) up to the time of their leader Moses and also include the Laws—guidance from God about how to live.

● The books of the **Prophets** tell the later history of the Jewish people and God's messages given to them through the prophets.

● **The Writings** include a variety of other books. One is the book of *Psalms*, which is a collection of religious poems and songs.

Reading the Torah

The Jewish Torah is written on scrolls like these. The scrolls are kept in a special cupboard in a Jewish synagogue—the ark. Jewish children are taught to read their scriptures in Hebrew (◊7).

Written treasure

Nearly two thousand years ago, some Jews wanted to protect their holy writings from the Roman army that was conquering their land. They pushed their precious scrolls—including scrolls of scripture—into pottery jars and then hid them in caves in the surrounding cliffs. The zeal of these people (who lived at Qumran in Israel) is one striking example of how much people of faith treasure their holy books.

✝ The Christian Bible

The Christian Bible has two sections, called the Old Testament and the New Testament. The word 'testament' means 'promise' or 'agreement'. The Old Testament is made up of the 39 books of the Jewish Tenakh. The New Testament contains 27 books:

● Four 'gospels' which tell people about Jesus. 'Gospel' means 'good news'.

● The *Acts of the Apostles* which tells the story of the early followers of Jesus.

● Several 'epistles' or letters written to some of the first groups of Christians.

● A book called *Revelation* which is a kind of dream or vision about the time when Jesus comes back to earth.

Christians believe the New Testament shows God's new agreement: anyone who follows Jesus is one of God's people.

Bible reading

The Bible is read aloud in churches. Many Christians also meet in small groups to study what it means to them. In addition, they make time to read the Bible on their own.

The Qur'an of Islam

Muhammad, the Prophet of Islam, could not read or write. He dictated all the things told to him by an angel on Mount Hira to friends who wrote it down. That book is called the Qur'an and most young Muslims learn large sections of it by heart.

 Learning the Qur'an

These Sudanese girls are meeting for their Qur'an class. Because Muslims learn so much of their scriptures by heart (they try to learn all of them!) they can call to mind the teachings of their faith in all the day-to-day choices they have to make through life.

The Ramayana

Here is a traditional painting showing a scene from the Ramayana. Rama and Sita are being enthroned. Today, many Hindu children learn the story of Rama from comic books.

 ## Buddhism

There are many Buddhist holy writings. Indeed there are so many it is said that no one person has read them all!

The Holy Books of Hinduism

Hindus believe in a great power or spirit called Brahman. This Brahman (or 'God') has no form or shape but may come to earth and take the form of a god on earth. Some of the best known of these gods are Krishna, Vishnu and Rama.

One Hindu holy book is called *The Upanishads*. The word *Upanishad* can be very loosely translated as 'Sit down near your teacher'. *The Upanishads* teach that Brahman is present everywhere and is within all living things. Another Hindu holy book is the *Ramayana* which tells of the adventures on earth of the god Rama.

The Holy Book of Sikhism

The tenth Sikh Guru, Guru Gobind Singh, said that there would be no more human Gurus. Instead, Sikhs must turn to their holy book to hear God's teaching. The Book is called the Guru Granth Sahib and is treated with great respect. It is given the most important place in a Sikh temple (or 'gurdwara').

'Granth' means 'book' and 'sahib' is an Indian word meaning 'sir'—so what does 'Guru Granth Sahib' mean?

 The Guru Granth Sahib

The holy book of Sikhism is given a place of honour in the gurdwara (◊6). It is placed on a platform under a canopy. A special fan—a chauri—is sometimes wafted over it while it is read.

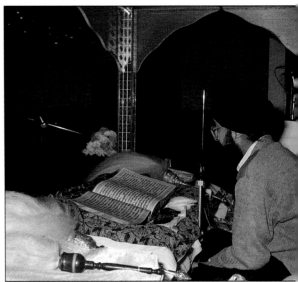

Welcome, baby!

In every country and every faith, families want to help their children understand the stories and traditions of their people.

Many people who believe in God say they belong to two families. One is their 'natural' family, the people they are related to. The other is a much bigger 'family' of all the people who believe in their religion.

In all religions, the birth of a new baby is a joyful time. Often, the whole natural family will come together to give thanks to God for the gift of new life.

✡ Jewish names

When Jewish children are born, they are given two names. One is an ordinary first name; the second is a Hebrew name, given in memory of an important relative. Two common Hebrew names are Moshe (which means Moses, ◁2) and Rivka (Rebekah).

In the family

Young Jewish children (right) wearing the traditional skull cap (yarmulkah) as they go to the synagogue. Already their parents have given them special names that link them to their own family and to the wider Jewish family.

✝ Christian baptism

There was a Jewish tradition of being baptized before the time of Jesus. It was a sign of accepting God's forgiveness for wrongdoing. One person who did this was the cousin of Jesus, John (known as John the Baptist).

Before Jesus started his work of telling people about God, he went to John who was baptizing people by dipping them in the River Jordan.

'But surely you have done no wrong,' said John. 'You don't need to be baptized.'

Jesus insisted—so John baptized him.

When Christians want to show they are joining the 'family' of all Christians believers, they get baptized as Jesus was. Baptism is a sign of a person becoming a follower of Jesus and in many families a new baby is baptized soon after it is born. The baby's parents promise to bring it up as a Christian.

Often, the family choose people they call 'godparents' to help them in this. Other Christians are baptized when they are older. This is because their family or Church thinks it is better for the person to wait until they can make up their own mind whether they want to be baptized or not.

In some church buildings, the person being baptized is taken into a small pool (the water comes up to their waist) and they are lowered right under the water.

In other churches, only a little water is used. The priest or minister uses it to make the sign of the cross on the person's forehead and then a small amount of water is poured over the person's head.

A baby is baptized

Parents, grandparents and older siblings watch in delight as a new baby is baptized into the Christian family. The picture in the window is of Jesus the good shepherd, loving and guiding those in his care.

Special gifts

A Christian child may be given special gifts to celebrate their baptism and encourage them in the faith. This collection of gifts includes a children's Bible and a gold cross.

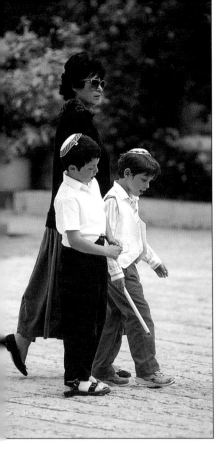

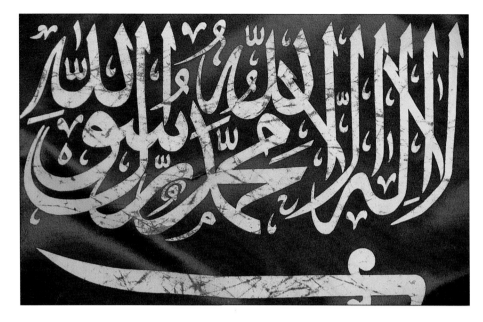

The shahadah appears like this on the flag of Saudi Arabia, the birthplace of Muhammad. The writing is in Arabic.

Buddhism

Buddhists say you cannot become a Buddhist until you are old enough to know what it means to say you are a Buddhist!

A Muslim baby hears about God

In a Muslim family, as soon as a baby is born, its father whispers into its ear: 'I witness there is no god but God (Allah) and that Muhammad is the Prophet of God (Allah).' So the very first words the baby hears are about God and God's Prophet. These words are called the *shahadah* (⟁13).

A Sikh family chooses a baby's name

Sikhs have a special way of choosing a name for a new baby. The Sikh holy book, the Guru Granth Sahib, is opened at any page. The first letter of the first hymn (or other writing) at the top of the left hand page will be the first letter of the baby's first name. To show they are members of the Sikh community—the Khalsa—all male Sikhs are called 'Singh' (which means 'lion') and all female Sikhs are called 'Kaur' (which means 'princess') (⟁2).

A Hindu welcome

When a Hindu baby is born, a priest or member of the family welcomes it into the world by whispering a prayer in its ear. The whole house is decorated with leaves and flowers to mark the happy event.

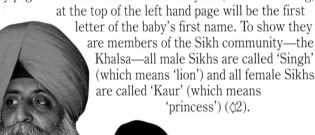

 Father and daughter

A Sikh father and daughter elaborately dressed for a celebration.

 A happy day

Bright flowers around the home tell everyone who comes that a happy event has taken place—a baby has been safely born in a Hindu home.

Full membership

What makes a person a 'grown-up'? And what do people mean when they say, 'You must be responsible!'? Some people have a party when they reach an age when they are legally 'grown-up'—when society says they can be responsible for themselves. The different religions of the world have their own ways of showing when their followers become 'grown-up members'.

✡ Bar mitzvah and bat mitzvah

A Jewish boy becomes an adult on his thirteenth birthday when he becomes 'bar mitzvah' ('son of the law') while a Jewish girl becomes 'bat mitzvah' ('daughter of the law') a year earlier on her twelfth birthday.

Up till these birthdays, they have been learning the laws of God: what is right and what is wrong. When they become adults, their behaviour is their own *responsibility*. Nothing *has* to happen but most Jewish families do celebrate at this time. Many of the person's family and friends will go to the Jewish meeting place, the synagogue, and the person will read or chant part of the Torah (◊3). Later there will be a special meal or party.

▧ Coming of age

A Jewish girl (surrounded by family and friends in the synagogue) reads from the Torah to show she is grown-up enough to be 'bat mitzvah'.

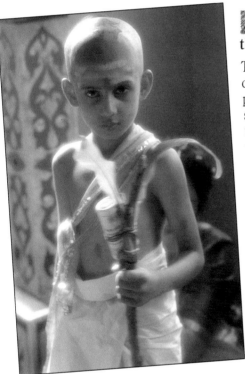

ॐ The sacred thread ceremony

This Hindu ceremony is performed on boys some time between their seventh and twelfth birthdays. It marks their entry into adulthood and is the most important ceremony in a young Hindu's life.

During the ceremony, the boy and a priest sit on opposite sides of a small fire. Prayers and hymns are chanted and then the thread is put on the boy. It is made in the form of a loop and is usually either red, yellow or white. It is worn over the left shoulder. As an adult Hindu, his responsibilities are now to:

1 worship God

2 respect holy men and holy books

3 honour his parents and old people

4 help the poor

5 care for animals and all living things

▧ Shouldering responsibility

This Hindu boy looks very serious as he takes on the responsibility of being grown-up in his faith at his sacred thread ceremony.

✝ Growing up Christian

People become members of the Christian church through baptism (◊4). When a person is baptized as a baby or a young child, there is another service (called confirmation) when they become 'grown-up' members of the church. They then make for themselves the promises their god-parents made earlier on their behalf. Often this happens when a person is between ten and sixteen years old.

The Roman Catholic church (and some other churches) also has a special celebration in between baptism and confirmation, when a child is seven or eight. This is to mark the time when they first join in Holy Communion (◊9).

▓ Confirmed for life

A Christian leader called a bishop makes the sign of the cross on a young girl's forehead as part of a confirmation ceremony.

☪ Islam

Muslims learn the duties of their faith at home (◊8, ◊10) and at the mosque throughout their growing years.

✵ Buddhism

As they grow up, some Buddhist boys spend a while living as monks (◊16).

▓ Saffron robes

Young buddhist monks wear traditional yellow robes. The colour is called saffron.

▓ Bowl of rice

Buddhist monks live on what is given to them—perhaps a bowl of rice as a whole day's food.

☬ The amrit ceremony

In Sikhism, 'coming of age' or entry into full membership of the faith happens with the amrit ceremony. This is when Sikhs become full members of the Sikh community—the Khalsa (◊2).

It takes place in a gurdwara and is led by five adult Sikhs (men or women) who wear special yellow robes. Before it starts, each young person makes a vow that he or she will dedicate him or herself to the way of life taught by the ten Gurus. Prayers are said and a hymn is sung. Then the five Sikhs stir sugar into a bowl of water, using a sword. A little of this holy water (called 'amrit') is poured into each young person's hands and some is sprinkled on their eyes—as a sign that they should see no evil. Then a little amrit is placed on their head. In this way, the most important parts of the body are made holy.

▓ Part of the community

All the members of the local Sikh community celebrate a young man's becoming a full member of the Khalsa at his amrit ceremony.

Members of all religions have special places where they can gather together as a 'family' of believers.

Usually these are special buildings in which they can worship God and pray to God. They often spend time and money caring for these buildings and making them attractive.

Hindu temples

A Hindu temple is called a 'mandir' (place of worship). Usually there will be statues of the different gods in it.

Almost every Hindu temple has a little bell. When Hindus arrive at the temple, they ring it to say that they have come to offer their prayers. They may also bring gifts of flowers or sweets for the god or goddess. (Later, these are given to the poor.)

This Hindu temple is in the city of Madurai in southern India, which is where Hinduism began.

Stupas, Wats and Pagodas

In India, a Buddhist temple or shrine is called a 'stupa'. In Thailand, it is called a 'wat' and in China and Japan, it is called a 'pagoda'.

Some are buildings you can enter; others (especially stupas) are solid—like monuments. Almost always there will be statues or carvings of the Buddha at the temple. Some visitors bring flowers or burn sweet-smelling incense to show respect to the Buddha. Others sit in prayer and sometimes there are processions round the temple.

Signs of worship

Flowers and candles decorate a Buddhist temple. Often, bundles of flowers and incense are available at the entrance. Worshippers can buy these when they come to offer their respects.

☪ The call to prayer

Muslims gather together to worship God in a 'mosque'. Many mosques have a tall tower called a 'minaret'. Five times a day, a man (called a 'muezzin') calls Muslims to pray to God (♭10).

In each mosque, there is a place where Muslims may wash before they pray. They also take off their shoes before entering. In the main prayer hall are mats on which Muslims can kneel and bow low to pray. When they do, wherever they are in the world, they face the holy city of Mecca. Most Muslim adult men are expected to attend prayers at the mosque at midday on Friday (which is the Muslim holy day of the week).

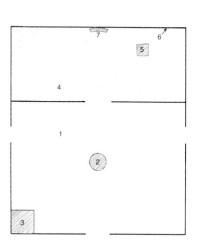

Towering minaret

From the balcony of the minaret the muezzin calls the faithful to prayer. They gather in rows and face Mecca to pray.

Parts of a mosque

1 The courtyard, which has several entrances.
2 Fountain.
3 Minaret—the tower from which the muezzin calls to announce times of prayer.
4 Prayer hall. This is often covered with fine carpets, on which the worshippers kneel to pray.
5 The pulpit, called a minbar.
6 The qibla wall—the wall which has the mihrab in it.
7 The mihrab is a niche in the wall indicating the direction of Mecca.

☬ The door to the Guru

A Sikh holy building is called a 'gurdwara'. The word means 'Guru's door'—the door to the holy book, the Guru Granth Sahib (♭3).

Everyone entering a gurdwara does so without shoes and with their heads covered as signs of respect to the holy book. During a Sikh service, the holy book is placed on a kind of throne at the centre of the gurdwara. It is kept covered except when it is being read. Behind sits the 'granthi'—the person chosen or elected to read from the book. The people also sing hymns and pray that they will be able to follow the teachings of the ten Gurus. A gurdwara is not just a place of worship. There may be classrooms where young Sikhs are taught their faith. There will certainly be a kitchen where meals are prepared because Sikhs always eat together after the main service of the week. This is a sign of the brotherhood and sisterhood of all Sikhs—but anyone is welcome.

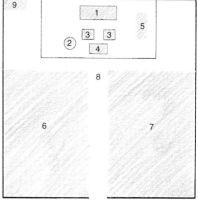

Parts of a gurdwara

1 The platform (takht) with a canopy (palki) above. The holy Granth is placed on a stool (Manji Sahib) on the platform, under the canopy, from where it is read. It is important that the Granth be visible from everywhere.
2 A basin of a sweet food called Karah parshad.
3 Gifts of food.
4 Gifts of money.
5 Place for the musicians (ragis).
6 Area where the women sit on the floor.
7 Area where the men sit on the floor.
8 Aisle.
9 Pictures of the Gurus.

7 Places of worship – 2

✡ Synagogues

Jews have special buildings where they can meet together and worship God. These are called 'synagogues' or (in some parts of the world) 'temples' or 'shuls'.

The most important part of the synagogue is a kind of cupboard called the ark. In it are kept the scrolls of the Torah (◊3). The ark is usually covered by a curtain. Above it hangs a lamp that burns all the time as a reminder that God is always present.

In the centre of the synagogue is a platform called the 'bimah'. It is from here that the Torah is read to the congregation. Jews come to the synagogue on important days in the year and also on their weekly holy day called the Sabbath (◊8) which begins at nightfall on Friday and continues through Saturday.

Because synagogues are meeting places for all the local Jewish people as well as being places of worship, they often have classrooms, a hall and a kitchen.

An informal gathering

This synagogue in Tel Aviv, Israel, is very informal, with men, women and children standing together.

✝ Churches, chapels and cathedrals

The buildings that are used by Christians when they meet together to worship God are called churches— but some Christians prefer to use the word 'chapel'. (The word 'chapel' can also mean part of a large church.)

A cathedral is the main church for a large area in which there may be lots of smaller churches.

Church buildings vary a great deal—old or new, highly decorated or plain— the important thing is that they are all places where Christians can meet together and worship God.

Many traditional church buildings are arranged like the one shown in the plan here. From the outside they are easy to spot because of the the tower or pointed 'spire' to remind people of heaven.

In others, the most important feature is the place from where teaching is given. These churches are often arranged with seats facing a central pulpit.

Yet others are arranged 'in the round', to emphasize the belief that all those who come to worship are members of God's family.

Around the world today, many Christians meet in whatever kind of place is available, be it a rented hall, a living room or simply an open space in their community.

Parts of a synagogue

1 The ark—a cupboard containing the scrolls of the law (◊3).
2 Seat for the rabbi.
3 Seats for grown-up men. A Jewish boy is considered a man after his bar mitzvah (◊5).
4 The platform (bimah) where people stand to speak.
5 Stairs leading to a side gallery.
6 Side gallery, with seats for women and young children.

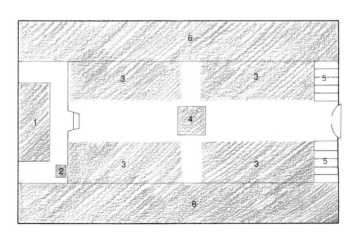

A focus for worship

This richly-decorated church in Turkey reminds worshippers of their belief that Jesus died to conquer death and evil. Beneath the statue of Jesus on the cross is the table from which Holy Communion is given—another reminder of Jesus' death.

The pulpit from which the teaching is given can be seen on the left.

Parts of a church

1. The table where Holy Communion is given. This table is often called an altar (♭9).
2. Chancel area, where the bread and wine used in Holy Communion are got ready by the leader (often called a priest).
3. Worshippers stand or kneel at the chancel rail to receive communion.
4. Choir area.
5. Fixed seats called choir stalls for the singers.
6. A raised stand called a pulpit, from which a talk or sermon is given.
7. A reading stand, the lectern, from where the Bible is read.
8. A likely place for a piano or organ.
9. Some large churches have side areas called transepts.
10. This whole area is called the nave, and is the place where the worshippers gather. Hundreds of years ago, it was usual to stand for the service. Nowadays, there are often seats in the nave.
11. Aisle.
12. The font—a large water container where new members of the church can be baptized (◊4).

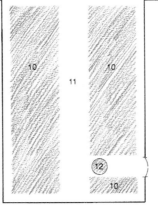

For Christians, the word 'church' has several meanings:

1 an *organization* (like the Roman Catholic Church or Methodist Church)
2 the *people* who are members of the whole worldwide church
3 a *building* for worship

The cross

The cross is an important symbol to Christians because Jesus was put to death on a cross. It has been used as the main symbol on this simply-built church in rural Kenya.

8 Family life

Religion is not something that only happens in churches and temples. For many believers, the home is a special and holy place.

✡ Shabbat (or Sabbath)

For Jewish people, the home is where 'Shabbat' or 'Sabbath' begins. This is the weekly day of rest which starts a little before sunset on Friday evenings and goes on till sunset the next evening. All meals are prepared in advance.

It is welcomed by the woman of the house lighting at least two candles and saying a prayer. Before the evening meal, the father of the family performs a ceremony called *Kiddush*. He takes a cup of wine and says a blessing. Everyone drinks from the cup. The father then blesses the day, his wife and his children. The meal itself then begins with the blessing of two special loaves of bread called *hallot*.

Family prayers

Jewish women say prayers for their family at the beginning of Shabbat.

ॐ Puja

For many Hindus, family life is very important and families tend to keep together—sometimes with grandparents, aunts and uncles all living in the same family group. Showing respect to older people is very important for Hindus.

In almost every Hindu home, there is a shrine. It may be a corner of a room where there are pictures and statues of the gods, decorated with flowers and fruit.

In the morning, it is usually the mother who goes first to the family shrine where she lights an oil lamp or candle and burns some sweet-smelling incense. Water may be sprinkled on one of the statues. Then the other members of the family may come and pray in a similar way. This saying of prayers at the shrine is called *puja*. Instead of performing *puja*, some Hindus will simply think about God—meditate—or perhaps read one of the Hindu holy books.

☪ A complete way of life

Family life is very important for Muslims and is often kept private from outsiders. Visitors to a home will be shown to a guest room and will meet the men and boys of the family. The women (and girls) will stay in another room for most of the time.

Muslim children learn about their religion by watching their parents and seeing how they pray five times a day (♪10). Although all Muslims must say these prayers at set times wherever they are, the Prophet Muhammad also told his followers that they should say part of their prayers at home every day.

Muslims often live in large family groups and members of the family help each other at all times.

Learning to pray

A Muslim girl prays, using the traditional postures of prayers she has learned from her mother.

A garden shrine

A Hindu family prepares fresh flowers each day for the shrine in their home.

✝ A Christian home

Christian parents spend time telling their children about their faith. Often they will read stories from the Bible and pray to God together. For younger children this may happen at bedtime.

In a Christian home, a prayer of thanks called a 'grace' is often said before meals.

The home is also a place where Christians from the wider church may meet to read the Bible and pray.

▓ Reading the Bible

A Christian family gathers round for the daily Bible reading.

✤ Following the path

For the Buddhist, the way you live your daily life (wherever you are) should be by trying to follow the Eightfold Path (◊13) and keeping the Five Promises or Precepts (◊15).

▓ The face of peace

Many Buddhists will have a small Buddha statue in their home. The peaceful face can help them in their meditation and their own search for peace.

☬ Traditions

When Sikhs live outside India, they believe it is especially important for children to learn about the traditions of their faith. Sikh children learn these at the gurdwara (◊6) and from their parents and grandparents.

▓ Learning the faith

A Sikh family makes a special visit to the main gurdwara in Delhi, in India.

9 Celebration meals

When people want to celebrate, they often have a special meal together. It might be a birthday party or a meal after a wedding. Followers of the different religions of the world have their own meals to celebrate events that are important to them.

✡ Passover (or Pesach)

Hundreds of years ago, before the Jewish people were first given their own land, they had to live as slaves in Egypt. They suffered in many ways but God promised to rescue them. Their escape began one night when many Egyptian children died but Jewish children were spared or 'passed over'. The Egyptians said the Jews could leave the country—and this they did, in a great hurry.

Once a year, Jews remember this and give thanks for their escape. They do this with a 'Passover meal' or 'seder'. It takes place at home and all the family and many friends are invited. In the middle of the table is the seder plate. The meal begins with the father saying a prayer, then dipping parsley in salt water and giving it to everyone. He breaks a matzot in two and shares one piece among everyone. Then a child has to ask a question: 'Why is this night different from all other nights?' And the father tells the story of the escape from Egypt.

▨ **A Seder plate**
The traditional Seder plate used at the Passover has a special place for all the special foods:

Matzot or unleavened bread: the Jews left in a hurry and did not have time to bake yeast bread

Roasted shank-bone of lamb: they ate lamb on their last night in Egypt

An egg: a symbol of new life in the new land

Parsley or lettuce: Passover is a springtime festival

Bitter herbs (usually horseradish): a reminder of the bitterness of their slavery in Egypt

Haroset (a mixture of apples, nuts and cinnamon spice): looks like the mortar they used to make bricks for the Egyptians but tastes sweet like freedom

Salt water: a reminder of the tears they shed during their suffering

✝ Holy Communion

After Jesus had spent three years travelling round Palestine, teaching and healing people, he and his twelve closest friends (his disciples) went to spend Passover week in Jerusalem (✡18).

At supper on the Thursday, he broke bread and shared it with his disciples in the traditional way. But he said something new. 'This is my body which is given for you,' he said. 'Do this in memory of me.' After supper, he took the wine and gave it to them, saying: 'Drink this, all of you. This is my blood which is shed for you and for many for the forgiveness of sins. Do this in memory of me.' The disciples didn't really understand what he meant. But the next day he was killed by his enemies—his body was broken and his blood was shed. Later, when they say him alive again, it began to make sense. Somehow Jesus had died for their wrongdoing and offered them forgiveness and a new life. Remembering and sharing in that meal became very important as a way of showing they accept his offer of forgiveness.

Communion has become (for many Christians) the most important part of their church services, in which they receive a little piece of bread or a wafer and a sip of wine in his memory.

This service is known by many different names, including the Last Supper, the Breaking of Bread, the Eucharist and the Mass.

▨ A Christian church leader called a priest gives a wafer to a girl during the mass. For these Christians, the wafer is the 'body of Christ'.

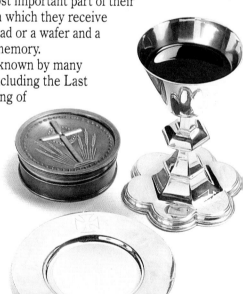

▨ A communion wafer on a silver patten and communion wine in a silver chalice. This is one traditional way of serving communion.

☬ Sikhism

Every week, Sikhs eat a special meal together in the gurdwara (◊6). When a community meets together they can more easily help and encourage each other.

▓ Serving one another

Everyone takes their turn at serving the weekly meal in the Sikh gurdwara.

 An Indian feast

Traditional foods are served as part of a Hindu feast.

ॐ Hinduism

Hindus have feasts and exchange sweets with each other at festival times.

✹ Buddhism

Buddhists do not have special 'holy' meals in the way Jews and Christians do—but they sometimes offer food to a statue of the Buddha as a way of showing they honour the Buddha.

☾ Islam

One time in the year when Muslims share a special meal together is at the end of the month of Ramadan (◊16). This is an occasion for a very special and happy family feast.

 Breaking the fast

A Muslim family shares a night-time meal that breaks the Ramadan fast. After a long and tiring day with nothing to eat, the food is especially welcome.

10 In the name of God

Followers of all religions say prayers to God. Prayer includes talking to God, listening to God, and spending time with God. Sometimes people pray in groups, sometimes alone. Sometimes they use their own words for spoken prayers. At other times they use 'set' forms of prayer.

✝ Teach us to pray

Jesus himself prayed to God and he expected his followers to pray. Once, they asked him to teach them how to pray. Jesus told them a prayer to say and this has become know as the 'Lord's Prayer 'or 'Our Father'.

Our Father, which art in heaven,
Hallowed be thy Name.
Thy kingdom come.
Thy will be done,
in earth as it is in heaven.
Give us this day our daily bread.
And forgive us our trespasses,
As we forgive them that trespass against us.
And lead us not into temptation;
But deliver us from evil:
For thine is the kingdom,
The power and the glory,
For ever and ever. Amen.

▨ Kneeling to pray

When Christians set aside special time for prayer they often kneel—as this family are doing at the chancel rail in their local church.

The prayer Jesus taught is the starting point for the different types of prayer Christians use:

● to *praise* God for who God is

● to *thank* God for the good things of life

● to *confess* or say 'sorry' for wrongdoing (or trespasses)

● to *ask* God to help them

● to *ask* God to help others

Jesus taught that God always hears people when they pray and that God answers in the way God thinks best.

✡ Prayers to the Lord God of Israel

Jews say prayers both privately and at religious celebrations. Their scriptures contain many prayers (which today are used by both Jews and Christians) and they also have many other traditional prayers.

▨ Praying at the temple

Jews believe that God hears their prayers anywhere. However, the most special place of all to pray is at the one remaining wall of the ancient temple in Jerusalem (the Western Wall).

▨ Notes to God

Every crevice in the Western Wall that can be reached is crammed with bits of paper on which people have written prayers. Writing down their request gives them confidence that God will not forget their prayer.

▨ Prayer shawl

A traditional Jewish prayer shawl has long tassels in each corner and words from God's law woven into the design of the cloth. Jewish men sometimes wear these over their heads when they pray.

☪ Salat

One of the five duties of Islam (♢13) is prayer, known as 'salat'. The Muslim holy book, the Qur'an, repeatedly says how important it is to pray at fixed times.

 Prayers through the day

Faithful Muslims stop work for prayer wherever they are. These Sudanese Muslims turn their attention from their flocks to their God.

Muslims pray five times a day: between the first sign of daylight and sunrise; just after midday; just after the middle of the afternoon; after sunset; and lastly when it is dark. These prayers may be said in a mosque (♢5) or at home (♢8), but Muslims can pray anywhere—provided they have first made themselves clean. Wherever they are, Muslims must face in the direction of the holy city of Mecca. When they are ready, they put down a prayer mat before they say their prayers in Arabic. A different position is taken for each part of the prayer. First, the Muslim stands—a sign of listening to God. Then the person bows to show respect to God. Next, the person bows low twice, touching the ground with forehead, knees, nose and palms—a sign of obedience to the will of God. Between each of these low bows, the person sits back on his or her heels. Special words are said at each point. All the movements are repeated two, three or four times according to the time of day. Muslims also say their own private prayers in their own language.

The Exordium

(The opening words of the Qur'an)

In the name of God,
The Compassionate,
The Merciful,
Praise be to God, Lord of Creation,
The Compassionate,
The Merciful,
King of Judgement Day!
You alone we worship and to
You alone
We pray for help.

ॐ Hinduism

Hindus call their way of praying *puja* (♢8). It will often take place at the shrine in the home.

Incense

These Hindu incense sticks burn to give off a sweet fragrance. It is a reminder that prayer, though invisible as the smoke, has a real effect in the world.

☬ Sikhism

Sikhs start each day by praying and remembering that God made everything. Some Sikhs use beads when they pray, saying God's name as they finger each bead.

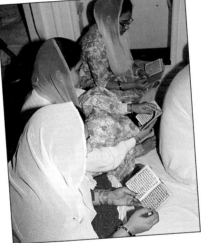

Sikh women at prayer

☸ Buddhism

Buddhists do not believe in a divine being called God but they do believe in something 'uncreated, timeless and formless'. Because they do not believe in God, they do not say prayers to God. But some Buddhists do say prayers to the 'spirit of the Buddha' which they believe is in each of us.

Prayer flags

Flags adorn a Buddhist shrine in Kathmandhu, Nepal. The flags fluttering in the breeze are a reminder of the belief that there is something invisible that affects the visible world.

11 Festivals of faith

All religions have special or holy days to remind people what is important about their faith.

	JANUARY	FEBRUARY	MARCH	APRIL	MAY	JUNE
CHRISTIANITY The Christian year focuses on the life of Jesus	EPIPHANY Wise men from other lands visit the baby Jesus and recognise he is a special person for all	ASH WEDNESDAY Christians make time to say sorry for wrongdoing	LENT Jesus spends time preparing for his work of telling people about God. Christians spend time learning more about their faith.	HOLY WEEK Jesus' last week in Jerusalem GOOD FRIDAY Jesus is crucified EASTER DAY Jesus rises from the dead (◊18)	ASCENSION DAY Jesus returns to heaven	PENTECOST (or WHITSUN) The Holy Spirit comes to the first Christians
JUDAISM			PURIM A joyful festival to remember when Queen Esther saved the Jews from being killed	PASSOVER A time to remember the escape from slavery (◊9)		SHAVUOT A festival to mark the giving of the Law
SIKHISM	GURU GOBIND SINGH'S BIRTHDAY		BAISAKHI The founding of the Khalsa			
BUDDHISM			THE WATER FESTIVAL A time for fresh starts		WESAK A time to remember the Buddha's birth, enlightenment and death	
HINDUISM	SARASWATI PUJA A time to honour the goddess Saraswati who helps people to understand things		HOLI A spring festival in honour of Krishna			

ISLAM has its own calendar. It has twelve months but each is only 29 or 30 days long (the time between one new moon and the next).

So Muslim years are usually eleven days shorter than other people's years. This means that Muslim holy days 'move' through the calendar used in western countries.

Muslim months

Muharram

Safar

Rabi' al-Awwal (sometimes called Rabi I)
Rabi' ath-Thani (sometimes called Rabi II)
Jamadi al-Awwal (sometimes called Jamadi I or Jumad I)
Jamadi al-Akhir (sometimes called Jamadi II or Jumad II)
Rajab
Sha'ban
Ramadan (◊16)
Shawwal
Dhul-Qa'da
Dhul-Hijja

Festivals

1st: Day of Hijra (marks the Prophet's journey to Medina)
10th: (marks the Israelites' escape from Egypt) (◊9)

12th: Day of the Prophet

Eid-ul-Fitr (◊16)

Pilgrimage to Mecca (◊17)

JULY	AUGUST	SEPTEMBER	OCTOBER	NOVEMBER	DECEMBER

ALL SAINTS DAY
A time to remember all good people who have lived in the past

ADVENT
Waiting for Jesus

CHRISTMAS
Jesus is born (◊12)

ROSH HASHANAH
Jewish New Year

YOM KIPPUR
A day of prayers for forgiveness

HANUKKAH
A family festival which celebrates the survival of Judaism (◊12)

GURU NANAK'S BIRTHDAY

DIVALI
Sikh New Year

FESTIVAL OF THE TOOTH
Once a year, in Sri Lanka, there is a procession when a casket (said to contain a tooth of the Buddha) is paraded through the streets.

FLOATING CANDLE FESTIVAL
(◊12)

DURGA PUJA
A time to honour the goddess Durga who protects the weak

DIVALI
Hindu New Year (◊12)

12 Festivals of light

Divali

Divali lights shine from every available ledge on this Hindu home.

People who believe in God, whatever their religion, often feel that their belief helps to make sense of what goes on in the world. Their faith is, for them, like a light shining in a dark place. It takes away fear, brings comfort and gives courage.

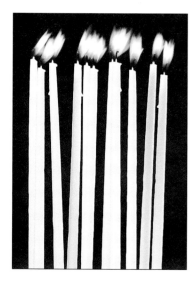

Light in the dark

Candle flames shed light in the dark. They are a symbol of hope in several of the world's faiths.

A row of lights

Divali is a Hindu festival which (depending on the date of the new moon) happens in either late October or early November.

The word 'Divali' means 'row of lights'. Hindus believe in one great power called Brahman (◊3). The aim of every Hindu is to become so good that they become part of Brahman. They are helped to do this by the gods and goddesses of Hinduism. Two are connected with Divali.

Lakshmi is the goddess of wealth. Many Hindus believe that, once a year, at Divali, she visits every home where a row of lights are burning—and brings good luck to that family.

Vishnu is the god who protects people from danger. Hindus believe he once came to earth as Rama, a warrior and king. Rama was married to the beautiful Sita (◊3). Once, she was kidnapped by a wicked demon. After many adventures, Rama rescued her. As Rama and Sita returned home, everyone lit candles and lamps and put them in their windows to welcome them back.

So Divali is a time for lighting lamps and candles to attract Lakshmi and to welcome the Lord Protector Vishnu.

Happy Christmas!

Christmas celebrates the birth of Jesus about 2,000 years ago in a little town called Bethlehem. He is sometimes called 'the light of the world' because Christians believe he brought happiness and light into a world that seemed dark and worrying.

Because he 'saved' the world in this way, he is sometimes also called the Saviour. Christmas is very important for Christians because, each year, it is a time to remember their belief that God chose to come to earth as a man. God's coming as a man is called 'incarnation'.

Light of the world

This is a Christingle, a traditional gift for children to remind them of several important Christian beliefs: the orange stands for the world God made, and the fruits are the good things it provides. The red ribbon is a reminder that Jesus' blood was shed when he died to conquer death. His life is like the candle: a light for the world.

The Christmas story

This is a traditional Christian crib scene, retelling the Christmas story—the story of Jesus' birth. Here is a model of the stable where (according to the story) Jesus was born and laid in a manger. His mother Mary and her husband Joseph watch over him. Shepherds have come to see the baby, having been told by angels where they will find God's special king.

Children light the last of their Hanukkah candles. They have a traditional multi-branched candlestick—the *hanukkiyah*.

☬ A Sikh celebration

Divali is also an important time for Sikhs. It is when they celebrate the release of one of their Gurus, Harogobind, from captivity.

☸ Buddhism

In November, Buddhists celebrate the end of the rainy season of the year with the Floating Candle Festival. Little 'cups' are made out of leaves. A candle is placed in each and they are lit and floated on a river. 'If you follow the light of Buddhism, you will be carried across the river of ignorance to the land of truth.'

✡ The feast of lights

In December, Jews celebrate Hanukkah, the 'feast of lights'. It remembers a time when the Jews won their protest not to worship the gods of foreigners who ruled their land. They made their temple a place dedicated only to their God.

The festival lasts eight days. On the first day, the special small candle is lit and then the first big candle is lit from it while a prayer is said. On each of the following nights, one more candle is lit. Hanukkah (sometimes spelt Chanukkah) is a time for parties and games and happiness.

☪ The lights of Islam

For Muslims, the stars and the moon are their 'guiding lights' (◊1).

◼ **Floating candles**

Simple leaf cups will help these candles to float on a river in the Buddhist Floating Candle Festival.

13 I believe...

Most religions find it helpful to have a 'creed': a statement that sums up what the followers of that religion all believe. The word comes from a Latin word *credo* which means 'I believe'.

✝ The Christian creed

This Christian creed has been said for 1,600 years—and is still said today in many churches.

It states their belief in one God known in three ways: the 'father'—and maker; the 'son'—Jesus; the 'Holy Spirit'—God in every believer helping and encouraging them. This three-in-oneness is called the Trinity.

Picturing God

This fifteenth-century picture from Cyprus depicts God in three ways: as Father, son and Holy Spirit. The dove is the symbol for the Holy Spirit.

I believe in God, the Father almighty,
creator of heaven and earth.
I believe in Jesus Christ, his only Son, our Lord.
He was conceived by the power of the Holy Spirit
and born of the Virgin Mary.
He suffered under Pontius Pilate,
was crucified, died, and was buried.
He descended to the dead.
On the third day he rose again.
He ascended into heaven,
and is seated at the right hand of the Father.
He will come again to judge the living and the dead.
I believe in the Holy Spirit,
the holy catholic (worldwide) Church,
the communion of saints,
the forgiveness of sins,
the resurrection of the body,
and the life everlasting. Amen.

✳ The Four Noble Truths

The Buddha taught his followers that people must face up to what are called 'The Four Noble Truths':

1 In this world, nothing lasts. Even the happiest moments pass away. There cannot be permanent happiness. The Buddhist word for the 'unsatisfactoriness' of life is *dukkha* (a word which means 'restlessness' or 'suffering').

2 *Dukkha* happens because people want more and more things and are never satisfied. They become greedy and selfish.

3 But *dukkha* can cease if you overcome your selfishness, greed and hatred.

4 The way to do this is to follow the Eightfold Path.

A water lily rooted in mud and slime unfolds pure white petals to the sun. This picture helps explain the Buddhist belief that the unsatisfactory nature of this world can be a starting point for reaching upwards to peace and contentment.

The Eightfold Path

If you are to follow the Eightfold Path, you must take eight steps. That is, you must try to do eight things in the right or proper way. (The eight-spoked wheel of Buddhism is one way of picturing them.)

● **Understanding** *People should see clearly what they are doing with their life.*

● **Thought** *They should not waste time day-dreaming.*

● **Speech** *When they talk, they should say good things, not bad or cruel things.*

● **Deeds** *Good deeds are unselfish ones; people must not be selfish.*

● **Work** *People should try not to take jobs which will harm other living creatures.*

● **Effort** *People should try their best at all times.*

● **Mindfulness** *People should pay full attention to what they are doing.*

● **Concentration** *People should try to concentrate on what they have to do.*

ੴ There is only one God.

ਸਤਿ ਨਾਮੁ Truth is his name.

ਕਰਤਾ ਪੁਰਖੁ He is the creator.

ਨਿਰ ਭਉ He is without fear.

ਨਿਰ ਵੈਰੁ He is without hate.

ਅਕਾਲ ਮੁਰਤਿ He is timeless and without form.

ਅਜੂਨੀ ਸੈਭੰ He is beyond death, the enlightened one.

ਗੁਰ ਪ੍ਰਸਾਦਿ ॥ He can be known by the Guru's grace.

☬ The Mool Mantra

The Mool Mantra shown here was the first hymn composed by Guru Nanak, the founder of Sikhism (◊2). It sums up the main beliefs of the faith. Here it is written in Gurmukhi (which is the name given to written Punjabi). The Mool Mantra is written at the beginning of every chapter of the Holy Granth.

ॐ Hinduism

Hinduism does not have a creed or statement of faith in the way other religions do.

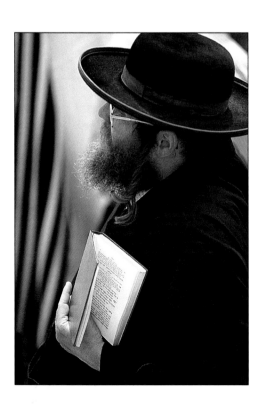

Studying God's word

This Jewish man longs to follow God's laws in every last detail—which accounts for the special way his hair has been left to grow, with a long ringlet on either side. Here, he earnestly studies the scriptures so he can better know and understand God's word.

☪ Shahadah

Muslims all around the world learn that the first duty (◊14) of Islam is to make a statement of their faith. This is done by saying the *shahadah* (◊4).

'There is no god but God and Muhammad is his Prophet.' In Arabic it is: 'La ila' ha illallah Muhammad ur rasulullah.' It is by saying this—and believing it—that a person becomes a Muslim.

Learning the faith

A Muslim boy learns more of his faith by reading the Qur'an, here resting on a Qur'an stand.

✡ Judaism

There has never been any one creed used by all Jews but there is a song called the *Yigdal* which is often sung at the end of synagogue services on the sabbath (◊7). It has 13 verses which sum up the main beliefs of Judaism. The first says: 'God, has, does, and will create everything.'

Knowing the law

Jews firmly believe that God's laws should guide them in all they do. This fragment of writing contains important words from God's law. It is shown actual size—small enough to be packed tightly into a phylactery (◊14). This one is almost 2,000 years old.

14 Right and wrong – 1

People who believe in God believe that God has said what is right and what is wrong. People need to live by God's standards.

War... poverty... sickness... the sadness and misery that make many weep also inspire others to work for what is good and right. People who belong to a particular faith often claim it is what they believe that strengthens them in the task.

✡ Laws in the desert

After the Jews escaped from Egypt (◊9), they travelled for a long time across a desert before reaching the Promised Land. Their leader at this time was a man called Moses. While they were in the desert, God gave Moses laws which the Jewish people were to keep at all times. These included the Ten Commandments.

The Ten Commandments

1 *You shall have no other gods but me.*

2 *You shall not make idols—something you worship as God instead of me.*

3 *You shall not dishonour my name.*

4 *I have made one day in seven a day of rest. Remember to keep it special in that way.*

5 *Honour your father and mother.*

6 *You shall not murder.*

7 *You shall not commit adultery.*

8 *You shall not steal.*

9 *You shall not tell lies about anyone.*

10 *You shall not covet anything which belongs to your neighbour.*

✝ Two great commandments

As a Jew, Jesus believed in and followed the Ten Commandments. Once, he was asked which was the most important one. For his answer he quoted the Old Testament, which gives this summary of the law:
'Love the Lord your God with all your heart, and with all your soul, with all your strength, and with all your mind. This is the first and great commandment. And the second is like it: you shall love your neighbour as yourself.'

Christians, like the Jews, agree that the Ten Commandments tell people God's standards. They are sometimes said in church services but more often Jesus' summary is used.

Jesus showed love for people—helping and healing them and spending time with them. On the night before he died, he gave them a new commandment: *'Love one another as I have loved you.'*

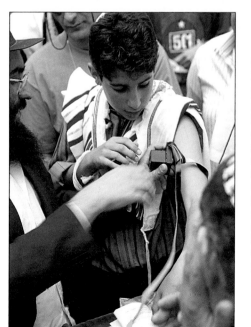

▨ Keeping the law in mind

In the Jewish scriptures God tells the people to bind the law to their arms and foreheads. Some Jews do this literally by strapping on leather boxes containing short extracts from God's laws. Wearing these boxes (called phylacteries) for religious ceremonies is a strong reminder that God's laws should direct what they think and do at all times.

▨ Love your neighbour

Caring for your neighbour is one of the most important parts of the teaching of Jesus and many Christians have tried to put it into practice by working with those who need help. Other Christians help by giving money to the homeless, the sick and the hungry.

Who is my neighbour?

A Jewish lawyer once asked Jesus, 'Who is my neighbour?' Jesus answered by telling this story:

'Once, a man was walking along the lonely desert road that leads from Jerusalem to Jericho. Suddenly, a gang of robbers jumped out from behind some rocks and attacked him. They tore his clothes off him, beat him up and robbed him of all he had. Then they went on their way, leaving him by the roadside, more dead than alive. After some time, a priest from the temple came along. As he got near the injured man, he crossed the road to avoid him.

Next, along came a man who helped with the temple services in Jerusalem. He looked at the injured man. Then he too crossed the road and left him.

The third person to come along was a man from the near-by country of Samaria. The Jews looked down on the people of Samaria.

When the Samaritan saw the injured man, he stopped, and got off his donkey. He took some wine and oils from his luggage and poured them on the injured man's wounds to clean and soothe them and then he bandaged them. He helped the man onto his donkey and took him to an inn. He booked a room for him and there he looked after him. When the Samaritan had to continue his journey, he left the innkeeper some extra money to pay for the injured man's keep until he was better. 'I'll pay any extra when I next come this way.' And then Jesus asked which of the three men had been a good neighbour to the man who was attacked.*

Zakat

Zakat is one of the Pillars or duties of Islam. It is the duty of giving money (or food) to the poor and others in need. Or money may be given to help with the building of a hospital or mosque—or even to help a poor student to study at a college or university.

Islam teaches that helping in this way is good for the person receiving the money and also for the person giving it: 'Those that do good works and pay zakat will be rewarded by God and will have nothing to fear.' The word 'zakat' means 'that which makes pure'. Zakat is paid each year at the festival of Eid-ul-Fitr (♭16).

Five pillars

Islam has five rules or 'pillars' which Muslims must obey at various times:

1 *Shahadah or making a statement of faith (♦4, 13).*
2 *Salat or praying (♭10).*
3 *Zakat or helping the needy (♭15).*
4 *Saum or fasting (♭16).*
5 *Hajj or pilgrimage (♭17).*

The debt

There was once a rich man and a poor man who owed him money. 'Sir, I can't pay you what I owe,' said the poor man, 'but, if you give me time, I'll pay you when I can.'

'Very well. Pay me when you can,' said the rich man. Islam teaches that this rich man will be rewarded by God for being generous. But Islam also teaches how much better it might have been: 'Sir, I can't pay you what I owe,' said the poor man, 'but, if you give me time, I'll pay you when I can.' 'You keep what little money you have,' said the rich man. 'Forget what you owe me: it will be my zakat.'

15 Right and wrong – 2

In our time, human greed has led to the destruction of much of the natural world. Many people are deeply concerned. For people who belong to any one of the faiths dealt with in this book, their concerns are coloured by their beliefs: whose world is it anyway?

 Buddhism

Buddhists often make five promises (known as the Five Precepts), based on the teachings of the Buddha:

Buddhists delight in all living things and treat them with respect.

1 *Not to kill or harm any living thing.*

2 *Not to take anything that is not given to you.*

3 *Not to indulge your body.*

4 *Not to lie or say anything cruel.*

5 *Not to drink alcohol or take drugs.*

Buddhist monks (and anyone living as a monk for a period of time) (♭16) make a further five promises or Precepts:

6 *Not to eat too much or after midday.*

7 *Not to be involved in, or to watch, dancing, acting or singing.*

8 *Not to use perfumes or ornaments.*

9 *Not to use a comfortable bed.*

10 *Not to accept (or even handle) gold or silver.*

A simple lifestyle

A Buddhist monk in a monastery in England eats a simple meal. Nothing about the monks' lifestyle is self-indulgent.

☬ Guru Nanak's teachings

Guru Nanak spent much time travelling around India, teaching people how God wanted them to live. He gave them a list of instructions to guide them.

Sikhs are also taught that it is important to help others; the Sikh word for this is *sewa*. It may be done by giving money or by giving up time to help someone without payment. A Sikh shopkeeper may give food for the weekly meal in the gurdwara (◊5). Others may perform *sewa* by running day-care centres for the elderly or some other type of community work.

1   *There is only one God. Worship and pray to the one God and to none other.*

2   *Remember God, work hard and help others.*

3   *God is pleased with honest work and true living.*

4   *There is no rich, no poor, no black and no white, before God. It is your actions that make you good or bad.*

5   *Men and women are all equal before God.*

6   *Love everyone and pray for the good of all.*

7   *Be kind to people, animals and birds.*

8   *Fear not, frighten not.*

9   *Always speak the truth.*

Don't...

destroy or injure anything

lie

steal

be envious

be greedy

Do...

keep yourself clean

be contented

be kind and patient

educate yourself

try to give your mind to Brahman (or God)

▨ Care for all creatures

Hindus have special care for all living things. Nothing should be hurt or trampled on.

ॐ Hinduism

Hindus have ten 'rules' for living. Five are things you shouldn't do; five are things you should do.

16 Putting faith first

Beyond

The tree is bare of leaves and through the branches gleams the golden sun. In a similar way, members of different religions believe that when they limit themselves to the bare essentials of everyday life, they have a clearer view of what lies beyond.

What would you find really hard to give up? Watching television? Playing your favourite game? Or what about giving up talking or even eating? If you ever try, you begin to see how much it means to you!

Members of the different religions sometimes try to go without food: that is, they 'fast'. This is not because they think that food is bad or eating is wicked. They fast for three reasons:

1 Going without food for a length of time makes them more thankful that they *do* have food to eat.

2 Fasting is a reminder that many people are too poor to eat whenever they feel like it.

3 Fasting is like an exercise—it is practice at deliberately putting things (such as eating) to one side to make their faith the most important thing in life.

☪ Ramadan

Ramadan is the ninth month of the Muslim year (◊11) and is special because it was the month in which the Prophet Muhammad began to receive the teaching of Islam from God (◊2, 3).

To remind themselves of this, Muslims fast each of the thirty days of Ramadan during daylight hours. They do not eat or drink (or smoke) from dawn until it is completely dark again at night. During this month, they should also say extra prayers and try to read the whole of the Qur'an. All adult Muslims should keep the fast but very old people, very young people, people who are ill and women who are pregnant or feeding a baby are excused.

✝ Lent

In the Christian year, Lent is the period of forty days before Easter.

When Jesus was about to start his teaching and healing, he first went on his own into the desert to fast and spend time thinking. Christians remember this during Lent and some Christians fast for part of this time by giving up luxuries. They may give money that they save to the poor and needy. They also spend extra time thinking about their faith—reading the Bible and praying. Not all Christians fast in Lent but those that do so feel it helps them to understand what Jesus suffered.

Eid cards

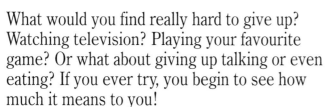

Eid-ul-Fitr

'Eid' means 'celebration'. Eid-ul-Fitr is celebrated at the end of Ramadan, on the first day of the next month, Shawwal.

It begins with an early meal. Then everyone puts on their best clothes and goes to the mosque. Afterwards, people visit relatives and friends to swap presents and to give each other sweets. People wish each other 'Eid Mubarak' ('Blessed be your celebration') and give each other Eid cards.

A Christian nun

A nun serves a meal in a school run by Christians for children in Panama, South America. Her plain dress and headdress are typical of the 'habit' worn by nuns.

Special promises

Some Christians choose to give up their whole lives to God in a special way. As monks and nuns they typically make three promises:

1 To have no things of their own.

2 To have no sexual relations with anyone.

3 To be obedient to God and to the group of monks or nuns they have joined.

Some monks and nuns live away from other people—monks in a place called a monastery, nuns in a convent. They spend much of their time in prayer and worship and in Bible study but they do other work—perhaps making things to sell to earn money for the convent or monastery. Other monks and nuns live 'in the world' and work as teachers or nurses or in other helpful jobs.

☬ Sikhism

Sikhs show their faith by performing *sewa* (◊14). They do not have any particular tradition of fasting.

Buddhist nuns

A small community of Buddhists in England gather round a simple shrine to meditate.

☸ Buddhist monks

Just as there are Christian monks, so there are Buddhist ones who also make promises (◊14). Buddhist monks spend their time in deep thought ('meditation') and live by begging. They may also work as teachers and help in building hospitals and schools. In some Buddhist countries, boys often spend some time (one to four months) living the life of a monk, in a monastery (◊20).

✡ Judaism

The most solemn day of the Jewish year is Yom Kippur which happens ten days after the start of the Jewish New Year. Jews fast for 25 hours and spend much of that time in the synagogue, praying for forgiveness for the things they have done wrong.

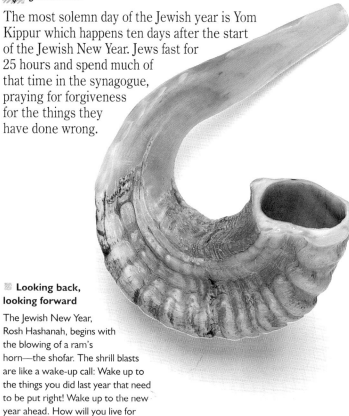

Looking back, looking forward

The Jewish New Year, Rosh Hashanah, begins with the blowing of a ram's horn—the shofar. The shrill blasts are like a wake-up call: Wake up to the things you did last year that need to be put right! Wake up to the new year ahead. How will you live for God?

ॐ Hinduism

Some Hindus give up everything—their homes, all they own—and become wandering beggars. They believe this will bring them closer to God. Such people are called *sadhus* or 'holy men'.

Holy man

Strange face painting and outlandish clothes... or skimpy rags... mark out the holy men of Hinduism.

17 To be a pilgrim

A pilgrimage is more than a journey to another place. It is a journey in quest of a deeper understanding of God.

Suppose you support a football team or have a favourite rock or pop group. You can watch them on television, you can read about them in magazines and (if it is a group) you can listen to their records. But think how much more exciting it would be to go and see them play!

People who believe in God know they can worship and pray anywhere. The buildings of their faith may be quiet places where they find it easy to think about God. But they can also go on journeys to distant places that are special to their religion. This kind of journey is called a pilgrimage. Some people find it brings them a deeper understanding of God.

The Holy City

Jerusalem is a holy city for members of three religions: Jews, Christians and Muslims.

☬ Sikhism

Sikhs often choose to visit Amritsar at least once in their lifetime. Amritsar is the Sikh holy city, built by the fourth Sikh Guru (◊2), Guru Ram Das, and is in the Punjab region of India.

Amritsar
The holy city of Sikhism glitters with gold.

☸ Buddhism

Many Buddhists make pilgrimages to places the Buddha once visited.

▨ This procession in Sri Lanka is being watched by thousands of Buddhist pilgrims.

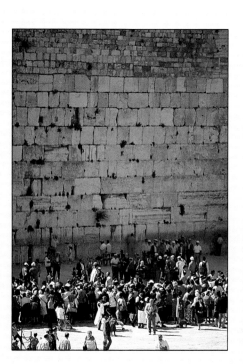

▨ **The temple wall**

For **Jews**, Jerusalem is the centre of the land God led them to and the place where King David made his capital city. There, David's son Solomon built a temple to God. All that remains of the last temple (◊20) is its Western Wall and all Jews hope that one day they will be able to go and pray there.

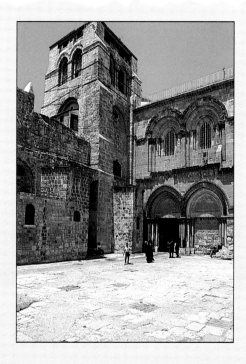

▨ **Where Jesus' body lay**

For **Christians**, Jerusalem is where the most important events of their religion took place (◊18). This is the entrance to the Church of the Holy Sepulchre, built over the place where many believe that Jesus was laid in a tomb, and therefore where he rose from the dead.

ॐ Hindu pilgrimages

A Hindu may go on pilgrimage as a 'thank you' for favours already granted but, as likely as not, the aim is to go to bathe in one of India's many holy rivers and have one's sins or wrongdoing washed away.

A pilgrimage is a joyful event, and sometimes a whole community sets out together. They meet friends, see the sights, wear new clothes and eat festive meals. There are many holy places to which Hindus make pilgrimages but the most important is the River Ganges. One of the greatest religious centres on this river is Varanasi.

▨ Varanasi

Varanasi is also known as Benares. For about three miles, the left bank of the river is lined with steps, known as 'ghats'. From these the pilgrims bathe in their thousands.

☪ Muslim pilgrimages

The fifth duty or pillar of Islam (◊14) is to make a pilgrimage to Mecca. The word for this duty is 'hajj' (which means 'to set out with a purpose').

The city of Mecca is in what is now Saudi Arabia. It was the birthplace of Muhammad (◊2). Muslims believe Mecca was important long before his birth. Here is the first 'House of God', and they believe it is the first place that the One God was worshipped by a man they call Ibrahim (and whom Jews and Christians call Abraham). This temple is now known as the Ka'ba. It is a cube-shaped, stone building which stands in what is now the courtyard of the Great Mosque. The Ka'ba is covered in a black silk and cotton cloth which has the words of the Qur'an embroidered upon it. Inside, the Ka'ba is unfurnished except for gold and silver lamps. Ordinary pilgrims do not enter: it is open only a few days each year for special visitors.

The Hajj

The Hajj is performed during the second week of the twelfth month of the Muslim year.

As pilgrims approach Mecca they stop to put on white pilgrim dress. The purpose of this clothing is to stress simplicity, purity and equality: nobody's wealth or status can be told from what they are wearing.

Pilgrims next enter the sacred area around Mecca, forbidden to non-Muslims. On entering the courtyard of the Great Mosque, they walk seven times round the Ka'ba. From the Ka'ba the pilgrims go to the two small hills of Safa and Marwah which are within Mecca. Between them is a spring (called Zam Zam) and pilgrims take water from it home to those too ill to make the hajj.

▨ The Ka'ba

Pilgrims dressed in special white garments circle the Ka'ba in Mecca.

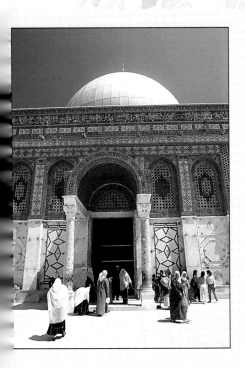

▨ For **Muslims**, Jerusalem is important because the Prophet Muhammad visited it once on a special journey. This golden dome is part of a mosque.

18 Life after death

Do you believe that, before this life, you were someone else? Or that when you die, you will live again?

Non-believers sometimes say that the idea of a life after this life here and now is simply 'make-believe', just a wishful dream or hope that death is not the end of everything. But those with a religious faith generally do not believe that death is the end of life. Believers say we each have a 'soul'; an invisible, inner part of us that lives on after death.

Buddhism

Buddhists believe that if people overcome greed and selfishness and so avoid all *dukkha* (◊13), then they will escape from this world and reach a kind of perfect peace.

Sikhism

Sikhs, like Hindus, believe in reincarnation.

'Western' religions ▶
The three 'western' religions (Judaism, Christianity, Islam) all teach that our souls cannot go into other people's bodies. They believe that each one keeps its own separate identity.

They also believe in a final reckoning when God will consider the good and bad each person has done, and bring justice at last. Some say this will happen for each person soon after they die; others say people 'sleep' until one final day.

'Eastern' religions

Hinduism, Buddhism and Sikhism have similar beliefs about life after death. All three say that (in some way) a soul returns to a different life on earth after death.

Hinduism

Hindus believe in 'reincarnation'. This means that after death the person's soul is re-born in another form of life. If, during their past lives, people have been *very* good, then they will go straight to God. But if they have done any wicked things, then their soul will go into another living being on earth. If the actions were very wicked then the person is re-born very low down the scale, perhaps as an animal. On the other hand, if they was only moderately bad the person will be re-born as a human being but at a humbler level in life.

People sometimes ask why should a child or someone who has not done any wrong should suddenly die. Hindus say this is because God is now ready to receive this pure soul and 'collects' it. But when 'innocent' people appear to suffer throughout their lives, Hindus say it is because of the 'carry-over' of sins from the past life, which must now be paid for.

A Hindu funeral pyre

This pile of wood will be set alight, so that fire burns up both the wood and the dead body. You can see the red-painted feet. Although the body will be turned to ashes, Hindus believe that the soul will be reborn in another life.

Ready for God

These Jewish graves are on the Mount of Olives—the hill that looks out over Jerusalem and the place where the Jewish temple once stood. It is considered a great privilege to have a grave in this place.

✡ Judaism

Judaism teaches that there is life everlasting after death but says little about what that life will be like.

✝ Christianity

When Jesus went to Jerusalem at the end of his travels round Palestine (◊9), he entered the city on a day now remembered as Palm Sunday. The crowds greeted him as a hero.

He taught in the temple. Crowds came to listen. But some people (including the chief priests) saw him as a rival and a danger. They plotted against him. On the Thursday evening, Jesus had a meal with his friends (◊9). Later that evening, he was arrested and put on trial by the priests. They had no power to execute him so they sent him to the Roman governor of the country, Pontius Pilate. The priests had now got the crowds on their side. Pilate was afraid they would riot if he did not do what they wanted so he agreed Jesus would be crucified. Jesus died on a cross that Friday. His body was put in a tomb. But that was not the end of the story. On the Sunday morning, his friends found the tomb was empty. Christians believe that Jesus came back to life and many of his followers reported seeing him. This is the main teaching of Christianity: Jesus died and came back to life three days later. A word sometimes used for this is 'resurrection'. Jesus showed his followers that death is not the end of everything. So Christians believe that 'through Jesus Christ' they are forgiven for their wrongdoing and that they have the promise of a new life as friends of God that begins now and continues after death. As the Creed puts it: 'the forgiveness of sins and the life everlasting' (◊13).

☪ Islam

Muslims (like most Christians) believe in 'the resurrection of the body': that is, one day after they have died, God will bring their bodies back to new life. Because of this, Muslims are always buried and never cremated when they die.

New life

Plants and trees seem to die during the winter but then burst back into life in the springtime. The new life of spring reminds Christians of a central belief: that Jesus Christ has died, is risen—and will come again one day to bring new life to all who follow him.

Once upon a time, each part of the world had its own religion and almost everyone in that area would follow the same religion. But in modern times, people travel much more than they used to. And sometimes they leave one country to live in another—perhaps to escape a war or perhaps to find work. So nowadays you can meet members of most religions in every country.

This map shows where each religion started and where most of its followers live. There are of course many more than six religions in the world. This map shows only where the followers of the religions described in this book live.

 Christianity

There are 1,000 million Christians in the world today. They all honour Jesus as the Son of God and try to follow his teachings but they belong to different groups of churches or 'denominations'. The main ones are:

The Roman Catholic Church
This is the oldest Christian denomination and its head on earth is the Pope (or Bishop of Rome).

The Orthodox Church
The Orthodox Church separated from the Roman Catholic Church in the eleventh century and was then centred on Constantinople.

The Protestant Churches
(which now include Methodists, Lutherans, Pentecostalists, Presbyterians and Baptists) began in the sixteenth century when they 'protested' at things they thought were going wrong in the Roman Catholic Church.

There are also the **Episcopalian Churches** *(including the Church of England) which is part-Catholic, part-Protestant.*

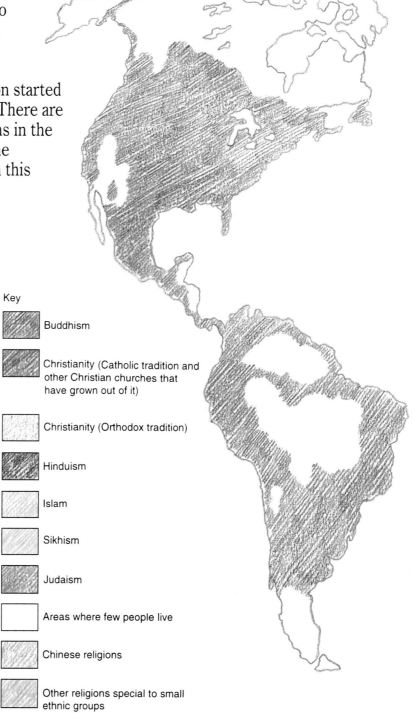

Key

Buddhism

Christianity (Catholic tradition and other Christian churches that have grown out of it)

Christianity (Orthodox tradition)

Hinduism

Islam

Sikhism

Judaism

Areas where few people live

Chinese religions

Other religions special to small ethnic groups

✡ Judaism

The Romans who ruled the Jews' homeland at the time of Jesus later became much stricter and crueller in the way they treated the Jews—and eventually destroyed the temple in Jerusalem.

To save their lives, most Jews fled from their 'Promised Land'. In the following centuries, they settled in many countries but were often ill-treated. Between 1937 and 1945, the Nazis (who then ruled Germany) killed six million Jews. In 1948, the Jews once again had a homeland when the country of Israel was created. Jews continue to live in other countries as well as in Israel.

☸ Buddhism

Bodh Gaya in India is the place where the Buddha learned the Truth (◊2). However, Buddhism spread to other eastern countries and there are now more Buddhists in these countries than in India. Buddhism is also becoming popular in European countries and in North America.

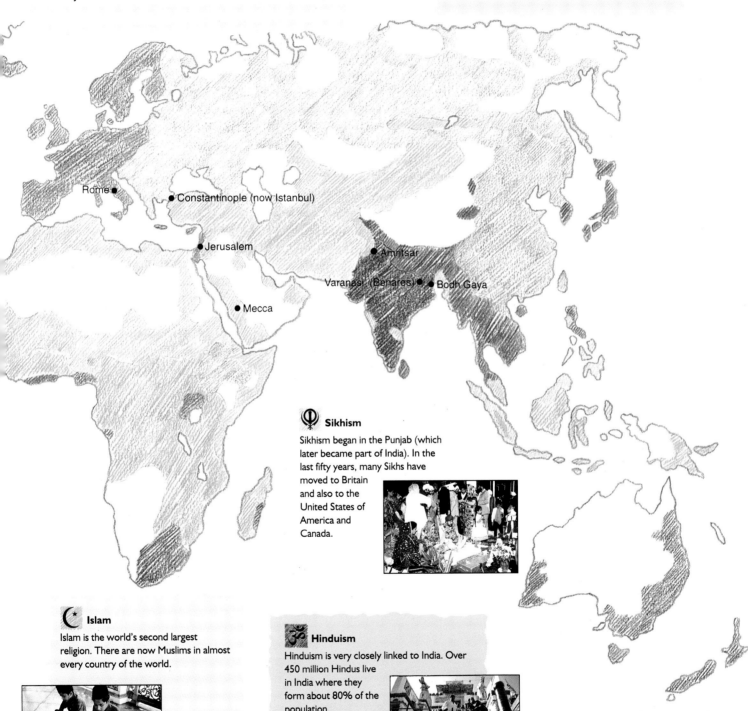

☬ Sikhism

Sikhism began in the Punjab (which later became part of India). In the last fifty years, many Sikhs have moved to Britain and also to the United States of America and Canada.

☪ Islam

Islam is the world's second largest religion. There are now Muslims in almost every country of the world.

🕉 Hinduism

Hinduism is very closely linked to India. Over 450 million Hindus live in India where they form about 80% of the population.

20 The meaning of belief

People can say all sorts of things are real because they can see them, touch them, hear them. People do not know God or their faith in this way. Instead, they have put their *trust* in something—and found that it makes sense of life. This makes them sure that their faith is something real.

For some, their faith changes everything—it becomes the centre of their life:

- They read the holy books of their religion.
- They pray to God.
- They join other believers to worship God.
- They become full members of their religion.
- They help those who need help.

Finding out about the great religions of the world can help *anyone* to work out what they believe. As well as learning *about* religion, we can learn *from* the great religions and the people who believe in them. The stories of the faith give everyone plenty to think about:

Muslim

'I live by Islam: Islam is my life.'

Being Muslim doesn't just mean I say prayers. Being Muslim means I help peop I have a duty to. It is an obligation.

Islam doesn't mean I can't play sports. doesn't mean I can't enjoy myself. But wh I'm out with my friends, I always know I a a Muslim so I shouldn't do things that go against the teachings of my faith.

Sikh

My sisters and I come to our temple each week. Its proper name is the gurdwara. We sing and say prayers and listen to people reading from the holy book. Then we all meet together to share a meal— just as if we were all one big family.

Guru Nanak and the banquet

Guru Nanak spent many years travelling around, teaching people how God wanted them to be kind to each other.

One of the cities he visited was Eminabad, which is not far from the Sikh holy city of Amritsar and is now in Pakistan. One day when Guru Nanak had finished teaching, a poor carpenter called Bhai Lalo went shyly up to him and invited him to supper. Guru Nanak accepted his invitation. But a very rich businessman called Malik Bhago also sent an invitation. 'When Nanak comes,' he said to himself, 'that'll prove to everyone that I'm a generous and good and popular person— just like him.' Which he wasn't: he was cruel to his workers, he was unfair and he was mean. Guru Nanak thought about the two invitations. At last he decided to go to Malik Bhago's house. 'But I shall take a piece of bread you have baked, Bhai Lalo.' As they sat down to eat in Malik Bhago's house, Guru Nanak took two pieces of bread, one in each hand. One was the

one that Bhai Lalo had baked; the other was from Malik Bhago's house. Guru Nanak squeezed both pieces of bread. Out of the bread that Bhai Lalo had baked dripped pure fresh milk—and out of the bread from Malik Bhago's house there came drops of blood. 'What does this mean?' asked Malik Bhago. 'It means,' said Guru Nanak, 'that I would prefer to eat Bhai Lalo's plain food which has been earned by his hard work and prepared with care by himself—rather than eat this banquet which has been made possible only because you've become rich by cheating the poor and by tricking those with whom you do business.'

Hindu

For me, the most important thing about Hinduism is believing your soul will never die. Even when your body dies, your soul will live on in another person. So you always have to try to be good.

That doesn't mean you can't have fun. I love dressing up in my best clothes and wearing special jewellery—as I did when my sister got married. She's wearing red because she's the bride.

Buddhist

I've become a monk! Yes, me! I had a big party and then I came here to this monastery where the grown-up monks live. It's not a strict place. I can play football with the other boy monks and my parents come on visits, but we have lots of lessons about what the Buddha taught. I'm staying here for just a few months. I may become a monk for good when I grow up. I don't know yet.

Christian

One thing I try to do each day is read a chapter of the Bible. Not just read it once. I think about it carefully and what it's telling me about how I should live my life.

Jew

I live here in Jerusalem. It's a very special city for all Jewish people whether they live in this country or not.

I like talking with my friends but today's Friday and the sabbath starts this evening so before then I'll go back home to be with my family. We always spend the sabbath together as a family.

Next week I'll be thirteen and it's my bar mitzvah. All my friends and family will be with me that day, when I make my promises in the synagogue.

Index